THE DUFFER'S
GUIDE TO
GOLF

A Second Slice

COLUMBUS BOOKS
LONDON

D1119797

Copyright © 1984 Gren of the *South Wales Echo*

First published in Great Britain in 1984 by
Columbus Books Limited
19–23 Ludgate Hill, London EC4M 7PD
Reprinted 1987, 1988

Printed and bound in Great Britain by
Redwood Burn Limited, Trowbridge, Wiltshire

ISBN 0 86287 165 4

CONTENTS

The Golfing Duffer

The golfing duffer is the player who counts his round in lost balls, not strokes.

The duffer zig-zags his way around the course, meeting up with his opponent only on the green, hours after they last met on the tee.

The duffer is the one who hits a divot further than his ball.

The duffer has been on more parts of the golf course than even the groundsman.

So, if you feel you, too, may be a duffer, this guide is for you.

Types of Golfing Club

It can't be stressed too strongly before you apply to join a golf club that not all are the same, socially or from a playing-excellence point of view. The duffer, therefore, is encouraged to take a careful look at the club to which he is ready to offer his body.

Basically, there are four types...

1. The traditional club

This is the ivy-covered, large country house type of club, where the average age is about five times the average handicap and where the club secretary has apoplexy every time someone motors up the long, shingled drive-way in a Datsun.

Almost all members are referred to by their former military rank, or their initials, as they sit around playing more bridge than golf, while out on the course it's very difficult to tell the lady members from the men.

There's not much chance of the duffer being allowed to join this club, anyway, unless he's filthy rich and related to the Archbishop of Canterbury.

2. The pretentious club

The worst of all golfing clubs, knee-deep in middle-management sales people, sipping Campari or chest-hugging their CAMRA-approved beer in half-pint, handled pots while they boast about their last round, knocking at least ten strokes off their real scores.

Duffers beware this club: you'll never get an afternoon game because the course is choked with trendy wives hacking their way about.

3. The social club

One of the best types of club for the duffer. The members here aren't too concerned about golf, only bothering to play a round when the bars are closed.

They are vaguely aware of some club championship—and they think there's a club pro somewhere. But no one cares too much as long as the beer's good, the company is pleasant and the steward's wife can cook up delicious snacks at midnight.

Duffers should seek out this type of club—their game won't improve but their social life will.

4. The 'If-you've-got-your-own-ball, -you're-welcome' club

This club is nothing more than an exaggerated pitch-and-putt course attached to an over-ambitious shed. Members happily thrash around the gorse and welcome, with unbridled friendliness, any visitor who cares to wander in. If the visitor should happen to have a post-1960 half set of clubs, he will immediately be made club captain.

The duffer would be well advised to join this kind of club. He'll be at home with all the other duffers there.

Types of Golf Course

Apart from the little hole that the ball is supposed to go into, golf courses have very little else in common.

The playing areas and conditions change more often than the average golfer's grip.

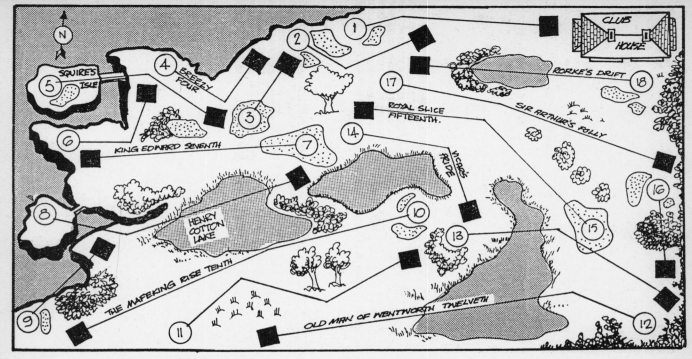

1. The royal and ancient course

This is the traditional course where tees and greens are linked by gorse and scrub, long fairways, huge sand bunkers, rocky outcrops, lakes or sea. All are waiting to trap the ambitious golfer – who on this type of course is always buffeted by at least a force eight, which doesn't do much for his slice but looks good on his hook.

Duffers should avoid this type of course unless they happen to be golf-ball salesmen.

2. The Campari-and-soda course

This course seems to have everything painted white: little fences, bottoms of tree trunks, and so on. Twee hanging floral baskets abound. The X!!**!! tree you've just sliced into again carries a botanical description. Ball-washers sprout like bullrushes near every tee, as do windsock direction signs and information boards. Beautiful oak seats are dotted around the manicured fairways for the members who come to gaze not at the golf but at the views. The duffer should not attempt to play here.

13

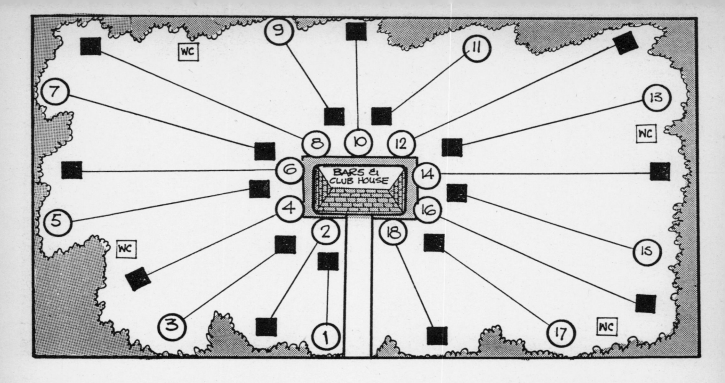

3. The urban social course

A marvellous course. Everything is geared to not being away from the club bar for too long. Dead straight, flat fairways with nothing on them that is designed to slow down the golfer: no sand-traps, no dog legs, trees or rough. The average for this type of eighteen-hole course is about 54.

The duffer should strive to find such a club and, when he does, take out life membership.

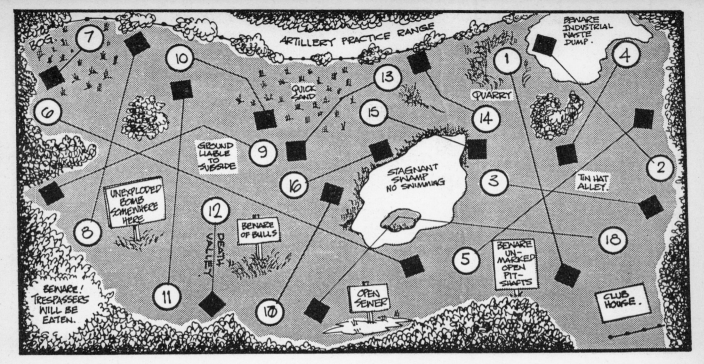

4. The 'this-time-last-year -it-was-a-flooded-meadow' course

This is a fairly basic type of course: the head greenkeeper is a sheep. Balls don't spin much, landing six inches deep in a bog.

Efforts will have been made here to make the greens playable. An area around the hole will have been concaved so that any ball landing within a three-foot radius of the hole will roll in. While at the tee, mis-hitting members have driven sheep droppings over two hundred yards. Duffers should have spiked wellies.

15

Golf Club People

Golf clubs may change but the members are always the same. The duffer should be aware of certain types before offering his skills to any particular club and be wary of the following people.

1. The club president

Usually a big wheel in the local community. Whatever it is that he is so respected for, it isn't buying drinks in the club bar.

A president can talk for hours without once saying 'What's yours?' or 'It's my shout'.

He doesn't often play these days, preferring instead to hope that time will heal the memory of what a duffer he was.

17

2. The club captain

Easily recognizable, he's the one who's always dressed as if he's about to attend a social function. His left hand holds a drink, his right is out-stretched, offering a warm handshake to everyone, member or guest (he's not really sure who's who).

The captain is always at least four drinks ahead of everyone (except the steward), and since taking office has hardly any time left to play golf.

He's usually a very nice fellow – if only he'd stop making speeches.

3. The club secretary

The secretary is very fussy, hard-working and paper-loving. He works at the club from early evening until very late at night on club business. Members think this is devotion to duty. It's not — he'll do anything to get away from his wife.

The secretary fusses over local rules, worries about memberships, gets cross over some of the notices that appear on the board, but really comes into his own at the club AGM, which he stage-manages. On these occasions, after hearing many committee chairmen praise him, he will yet again, with martyr-like selflessness, modestly allow his name to go forward for another year in office.

4. The chairman of the Ladies' Committee

The duffer should fear this member as much as the club greenkeeper.

The Ladies' chairman aggressively protects her members like a mother hen. She concerns herself with ladies' competitions, ladies' rights and ladies' powers within the club with all the vigour of an alcoholic in a brewery.

Duffers, beware this lady – she can outdrink you too!

5. The greenkeepers

All greenkeepers secretly hate all golfers. They see the golfers' sole function in life as to ruin what they have spent years lovingly perfecting.

To get job satisfaction greenkeepers, with un-bridled joy, delight in mashing up in-play golf balls, and chewing up expensive clubs left near greens each time they tractor-mow the fairways.

6. The club pro

The pro can change your game from that of an incompetent, slicing hacker into an ineffective hooking duffer (for a trifling financial consideration) while he dreams of the day he wins the British Open.

The pro pleasantly puts up with any player's shortcomings, welcoming each shortcoming as a bit more off the mortgage, while in his golf shop he can sell you all the latest gadgetry – to make you into an even better-equipped duffer.

Types of Golfer

All golf clubs have seven basic types of player. The duffer will do well to recognize these on sight and act accordingly.

1. The scratch player

This golfing machine plays only to win. He hasn't really enjoyed a game since getting to a single-figure handicap. He's first to enter every competition – even the Rabbits', which he enters under an assumed name. He's entered the ladies' competitions, too, and would have won but for his all-too-obvious padded bra bursting during his backswing on the ninth.

When he's not playing, he's practising his swing in the nets or expending an afternoon's concentration on the putting area.

He hasn't seen his wife or children since last summer when he took them on a golfing holiday.

Duffers should avoid this type at all costs.

2. The sales-manager type

This one is a strange type of club member. He will speak to you only if you're in the market to buy something from his range, and his game varies between average and terrible, depending on the size of the contract you may be able to put his way.

He's very unreliable – never plays in team matches, preferring to arrange his own games (where he is often seen whipping out his order-book instead of his putter).

The duffer could look good with this type – if he has purchasing authority.

3. The 'It-helps-to-pass-the-time-when-I'm-out-for-a-walk-with-the-dog' type

Usually a retired gentleman or a teacher on yet another day off. He potters around the course with only three clubs, playing the ball whenever he can remember where it landed. Nothing troubles him. He hasn't used a scorecard since 1956, at which point it struck him that filling it in seemed too complicated to be fun. Club rules mean little to him, golf rules nothing. He often gets lost on the course.

This type can always be recognized: he's the one on the fifth tee trying to drive his ball to the third green.

This type of player is a tonic. The duffer should offer to play against him whenever possible.

4. The 'Tell-me-which-one-to-hit' type

The club's playing drunk. He drinks only to calm his nerves before a round. Sometimes he gets so calm he can't talk properly, and often has to be pointed towards the next hole. He insists that local rules allow him to throw the ball fifty yards hole-wards over his opponent's left shoulder, should he have driven the ball into unplayable rough.

This type of player is usually good for five holes, whereupon he goes to sleep under a tree after asking the others to wake him when they return.

The club's playing drunk should not be confused with the club drunk — he's the one who collapses before he even gets to the first tee.

Duffers should avoid this type of player unless they can play him for money.

5. The snappy dresser

The snappy dresser never cares too much about his game as long as his appearance draws gasps of admiration from his friends.

Very often he looks so good that opponents watching him more than their game will be three down before they realize how poor his golf actually is.

The snappy dresser will never venture into any rough in case he ruins his shoes or trousers.

Duffers should always try to arrange games with the snappy-dresser type.

6. The equipment freak

The equipment freak is the chap who's the first in the club with the latest piece of golfing apparatus.

He is the golf shop's dream, happily buying anything that he considers will improve his game or impress other members. He could be a good golfer but he gets so worn out trailing all his equipment that he's shattered by the sixth.

Duffers should play this type only if they wish to buy a range of second-hand equipment.

Types of Golf Club

Although you have probably got a bagful of clubs, you need only four. The others that you have been lugging around the countryside, convinced that they make you play better, are totally superfluous and go to prove that golf-club manufacturers are the world's greatest con-artists.

Throw away all except the following four – and see how your game improves.

1. The belter

This is the longest of the clubs in your bag and is called the belter because it is used for belting snakes and frogs or, indeed, anything that may attack you when you look for your lost ball.

The belter is also useful for poking up drain-pipes should your magnificent chip shot have ended there.

Never try to hit the ball with your belter. It's made of wood and will probably break.

The duffer shouldn't worry about buying a belter until he has acquired the following three clubs.

2. The whoosher

So called because as you swing the club through the air it makes a nice noise. Even if you don't connect with the ball it can be very satisfying.

This club should be used if you hope to hit the ball a long way along the grass.

Duffers may also use this club to kill snakes if they haven't yet bought a belter.

3. The up-an'-under

This is the club that looks as if the shiny bit on the end has been bent backwards. Don't try to straighten it: it's designed this way so that when you swing it at the ball a slice of turf can be removed cleanly without disturbing the ball.

It's also useful for swinging in the bunker, where it can shower the green with sand.

But beware! If the ball is struck with the up-an'-under it flies almost vertically, gaining hardly any length.

Duffers, please note: it can also lodge the ball up a nostril.

4. The prodder

The prodder is the smallest club in your bag. It should be used for tapping the ball short distances, i.e. out of the club-house shower room on to the patio or from the back seat of a Cortina into the car park (whereupon a whoosher may be used).

During summer droughts it's also useful as a hammer to belt plastic driving tees into the baked clay.

A good duffer never goes without his prodder.

Types of Golf Shot

There are only three kinds of golf shot. They are as follows:

1. You've hooked it.
2. You've sliced it.
3. You lucky *!!*!!*!

1. The classic drive

In the classic drive the club favoured by show-off professionals is the snake-killing wooden belter.

The object is to hit the ball as hard and as straight as possible. Not only does this shot look impressive, but it keeps osteopaths in business.

Duffers should not.play this shot at all.

2. The 'My-tee-went-further -than-the-ball' shot

This shot is used by everyone from time to time. If you, the duffer, should use it, you are expected to:

(1) claim the ball fell off the tee just before impact

     or

(2) ask your fellow players if they felt an earthquake tremor too.

3. The 'Pass-the-grass-rake,-caddy' shot

This is a very tricky shot. You have to get the wedged ball back on to the fairway from the very long rough. Duffers, of course, will never be in the rough – a true duffer will have discreetly dropped a second ball three feet within the fairway.

4. The putt

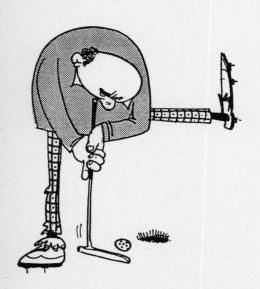

Use your prodder for this shot. The more ungainly your stance, the more impressive you look. Many golfers are considered great putters because they look like starved vultures hunched over their prey.

This shot is also known as the 'gimmie', because if the ball is putted to within six feet of the hole the duffer always enquires, 'Will you gimmie that?'

Taking Lessons

Golfers are always trying to improve their game. Whereas in most sports helpful instruction benefits the player's game, in golf, lessons appreciably reduce what little skill the player has.

Golfers strive to improve their game by one or more of the following methods.

1. Lessons from the club professional

These are always a waste of time because all the club professional does is to make you feel totally inadequate golfwise, showing off with grace and ease the shots that you, with monotonous regularity, fail to play. You also have to part with your money for this dubious privilege.

The duffer should never take lessons. They will spoil what little enjoyment he gets from the game.

2. Lessons from newspaper strips

Again, these are a total waste of time because they are so out of touch with reality. The drawings are always of well turned-out gentlemen playing in ideal conditions. Have you ever seen one showing how to overcome a 45-degree lie when you have one foot in a broken sewer pipe and the other sliding in some gooey stuff, while your club head is loose and there's a force ten hailstorm blasting away?

Duffers ignore such newspaper-strip advice. Anyway, it's impossible to have both hands on a club while holding a newspaper.

3. The video instructional film

Never try to use this method of help. It's even more humiliating than getting the pro to show you where you're going wrong. Now with a video you get your whole family telling you as well.

In conclusion, the duffer should not, under any circumstances, take lessons. They will spoil his game.

Helping Your Opponent Lose

It must always be remembered that duffers never win. Duffers' opponents lose.

With this in mind we offer the following tactics, which have been proven by some of the world's great duffers.

1. The 'This-is-the-one-you-always-under-hit' ploy

This statement should always be made when your opponent is half-way through his backswing, when he has been chipping well and he's within 100 yards of the green.

Your remark will destroy his confidence, and he'll smash the ball beyond the green into unplayable rough.

2. The 'This-is-the-one-you-always-over-hit' ploy

As for the previous ploy, except it should be used when your opponent is about 200 yards from the green, or on a very short hole.

3. The 'You-always-play-this-hole-so-well.-Very-few-actually-realize-this-green-slopes-left-to-right' ploy

On hearing this your flattered opponent, who has always played this as a dead flat green, will make new allowances and his sophisticated chip shot will run right off the green.

4. The 'I've-just-swallowed-a-bee' routine

This ruse can be used only once per round. Its success depends on perfect timing. Your opponent must be mid-way through his downswing, when you, standing behind him, let out an agonized scream. Clutching your throat, you collapse coughing, rolling about on your back with your feet kicking in the air. This will always result in your opponent's ball being smash-hooked square off the fairway. If you have performed this ploy well he will be unable to concentrate on any drive for the rest of the round.

5. The 'I'll-mark-your-ball-for-you' ploy

In this tactic you offer (ever considerate and sporting) to mark your opponent's ball as it lies within clear, easy putting distance of the hole.

Standing between your opponent and his ball, you pick it up and place the marker behind any convenient worm casts, sheep droppings or dents in the surface.

6. The 'sun-in-his-eyes' ploy

This can be used only on selected occasions, depending on the position of the sun. You, the duffer, should always have in your bag an iron with a blade that has been polished to a glass-like finish. This is used to reflect the sun, flashing it into the eyes of your innocent opponent as he's about to connect with his big drive or on his delicate chip or sensitive putt. It will successfully ruin any of these.

7. The 'Who's-playing-the-cheap-ball?' ploy

Use this highly successful routine when playing with a pretentious bunch of golfers – the more exclusive the club, the more effective it becomes.

It is used when all except one have teed off into the rough. You stride towards the only ball on the fairway and in a loud voice say 'Who's been playing the cheap reject ball?' Of course no one will admit to it and the pompous guilty party will happily lie about his ball being lost in the rough.

8. The 'cloth-tearing' ploy

Always carry a few pieces of linen in your bag, and when you are being continually out-driven tear one just as your opponent reaches the high point of his backswing. The resulting slice is a joy to behold.

9. The 'I'm-surprised-at-you-using-that-club-after-what-happened-last-time' ploy

This very simple routine is devised to ensure your opponent is never allowed to forget what a pratt he once made of himself.

As he's about to produce a delicate chip through the trees, over the lake or over the sand trap, you say gently: 'I'm surprised at you using that club after what happened last time.'

His confidence shattered, he'll be chipping into lakes, sand traps, or smashing into trees for the remainder of the round.

10. The 'lost ball' routine

Once again your partner will admire you for the considerate way in which you are helping him, as you both thrash about in the undergrowth after you have said something like 'I certainly saw it rebound left off that tree. It's near here somewhere.' Of course, it rebounded right — but you won't tell him that, will you?

This little scheme works well when your partner is chipping his way out of the long rough to the green, which he cannot see. You, ever eager to help, offer to stand as a marker in direct line between the flag and your opponent.

He's not to know you're standing fifteen yards to the left or right of the pin – and when he wonders why his ball is so far from the hole, you blame a sloping green or reveal that the ball was about to drop into the hole when it was picked up by a squirrel.

12. The 'You've-got-over-your-shanking-problem,-then?' ploy

This is most effective when playing a neurotic golfer — as he's about to go for his big drive off the tee. You casually remark, 'You've got over your shanking problem, then?' This will result in the most vicious shank shot you've ever seen. So ensure you are standing way behind him on this occasion.

13. The 'fore' ploy

This is the dirtiest of all ploys because it has very little subtlety.

Your opponent has just wound himself up to smash his drive at least 300 yards. As he is halfway through his downward swing you, at the top of your voice, scream 'Fore!' This will ensure his ball is wildly hit anywhere except on the fairway or any inbounds area. When your opponent stops crying you should of course apologise.

Course Etiquette

Good manners on the course are all-important. You must consider other golfers at all times, unless you are playing an 'away' course, in which case be as rude as you like.

1. Consideration for other players

Always shout 'FORE!' as your ball hits someone.

2. Bad language

Never call the chairman of the Ladies' Committee an interfering scrawny parasite unless she's within earshot.

3. Playing through

Always wait for players in front of you to clear the green before you drive off – unless, of course, their slowness is irritating you.

4. Sequence of play

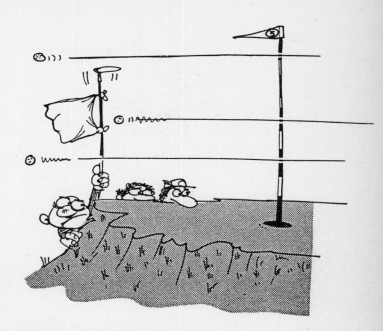

A two-player game has precedence over a four-player game unless one of the four players is an aggressive, bad-tempered bully.

6. Sand bunkers

Always rake over footprints left in the sand: failure to do so annoys following golfers. Another good way of annoying golfers is to hold barbecues on the greens.

5. Divots

Always replace divots — especially those you make on the green when someone is watching you.

7. The greens

Try to avoid bleeding over the area around the hole – it slows down the ball.

8. Gamesmanship

Gamesmanship should be discouraged at all times, unless you are losing.

Excuses

There are traditional excuses which the serious duffer should learn by heart. They should be offered whenever the occasion arises.

Excuse 1.

I did *see* him, but I thought it was a mirage.

Excuse 2.

I tried to play it off the club house wall.

Excuse 3.

Don't get stroppy with me, sunshine – I happen
to know you haven't paid last year's subs yet.

Excuse 4.

It wasn't me, captain! An identically dressed golfer played that one.

Excuse 5.

Nobody told me that was the Chief Constable
on the fifth.

Excuse 6.

I've over-compensated for the crosswind again.

Excuse 7.

Dammit, clear off! This is the Social Secretary of the Ladies' Committee and we're in a meeting.

Excuse 8.

I *have* paid my subs. I think the treasurer's on the fiddle.

Excuse 9.

I always play into the rough just here — it by-passes the dog leg.

Is that so? Sorry, I always thought that was *my* locker.

Excuse 11.

I'd love to but I've left my wallet in the car.

Excuse 12.

I didn't have this trouble when I was captain at Wentworth.